Dinosaurs by Design

DUCK-BILLED DINOSAURS

RANKING THEIR SPEED, STRENGTH, AND SMARTS

MARK WEAKLAND

BLACK RABBIT BOOKS

Bolt is published by Black Rabbit Books
P.O. Box 227, Mankato, Minnesota, 56002.
www.blackrabbitbooks.com

Jennifer Besel, editor; Catherine Cates, interior designer; Grant Gould, cover designer; Omay Ayres, photo researcher

Library of Congress Cataloging-in-Publication Data
Names: Weakland, Mark, author.
Title: Duck-billed dinosaurs : ranking their speed, strength, and smarts / by Mark Weakland.
Description: Mankato, Minnesota : Black Rabbit Books, [2020] | Series: Bolt. Dinosaurs by design | Audience: Ages 8-12. | Audience: Grades 4 to 6. | Includes bibliographical references and index.
Identifiers: LCCN 2018008463 (print) | LCCN 2018016999 (ebook) | ISBN 9781680728286 (e-book) | ISBN 9781680728224 (library binding) | ISBN 9781644660270 (paperback)
Subjects: LCSH: Hadrosauridae—Juvenile literature.
Classification: LCC QE862.O65 (ebook) | LCC QE862.O65 W434 2020 (print) | DDC 567.914—dc23
LC record available at https://lccn.loc.gov/2018008463

Image Credits

Alamy: De Agostini Picture Library, 20-21; Universal Images Group North America LLC / DeAgostini /, 22–23; commons.wikimedia.org: Zissoudisctrucker, 6; jameskuether.com: James Keunther, 12, 24–25 (dino); Masato Hattori: 4–5; nsf.gov: James Havens / National Science Foundation, 26–27; Science Source: Kurt Miller, 19; Shutterstock: 90miles, 13, 21; Arcady, 29 (scales); Catmando, 3, 7 (t), 10–11 (dino), 17 (both), 28 (l & r); Giedriius, 10; Herschel Hoffmeyer, 11 (bkgd), 14–15 (bkgd), 24 (bkgd); Kirasolly, 8–9; Linda Bucklin, 1; Lukas Uher, 16 (b); Michael Rosskothen, 7 (b), 16 (t); severjn, 28 (c); Skreidzeleu, Cover (bkgd); Warpaint, Cover (dino), 14–15, 31, 32

Every effort has been made to contact copyright holders for material reproduced in this book. Any omissions will be rectified in subsequent printings if notice is given to the publisher.

CONTENTS

CHAPTER 1

Duck-Bills by the DOZENS

The sun sets as a **herd** of duck-billed dinosaurs munches on plants. Two young ones chase each other. A mother quietly watches them.

Scientists have found many **fossils** of these huge animals. By the late **Cretaceous**, there were a lot of duck-bills. In fact, there were more duck-bills than any other kind of dinosaur.

Definitely Not Ducks

Hadrosaurs got the nickname "duck-billed" from how they look. Their mouths look like a duck's bill. But in most ways, duck-billed dinosaurs were nothing like birds. Their tails were stiff. Their lips were hard, not flexible like a duck's bill. Also, they had teeth. They used them to shred the tough plants they ate.

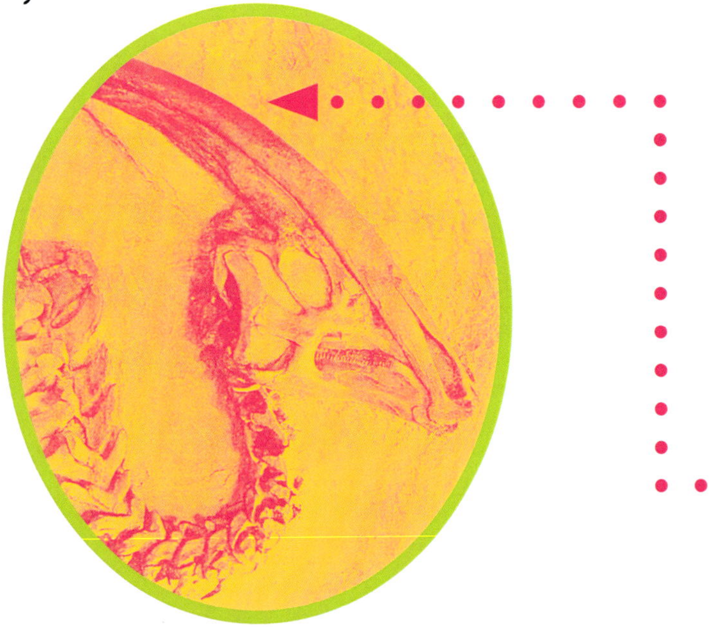

Crested Dinosaurs

Duck-billed dinosaurs can be sorted into two groups. One group had crests. The other group did not.

Some scientists think the dinos blew air into their crests. They would have made loud booming sounds.

The sounds might have warned other dinos that a predator was near.

Crests were made of bone.

FINDING DUCK-BILLED DINOSAURS

Scientists have found duck-billed dinosaur fossils all around the world.

KAZAKHSTAN
MONGOLIA
CHINA

CHAPTER 2

Compare the DINOS

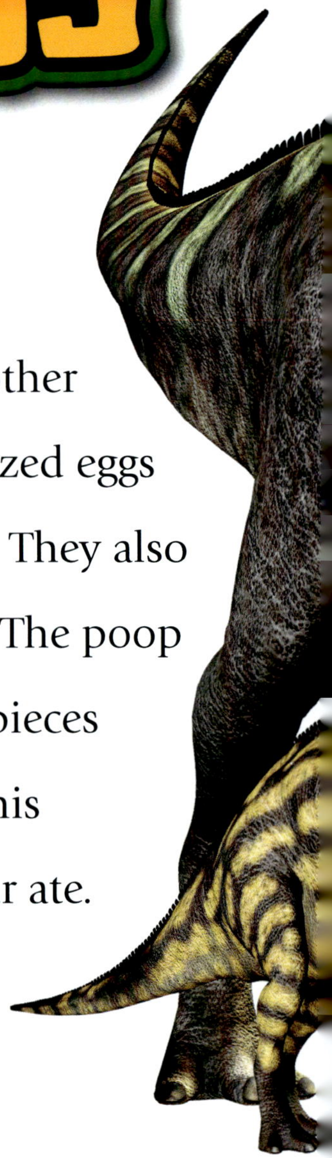

Maiasaura

(my-uh-SOR-uh)

Maiasaura means "good mother lizard." Scientists found fossilized eggs and babies with adults' bones. They also found fossilized poop nearby. The poop had pieces of wood in it. The pieces give clues about what plants this dinosaur ate.

FEATURE FACTS

LENGTH about 30 FEET (9 METERS)

WEIGHT up to 6,000 POUNDS (2,722 KILOGRAMS)

LIVED 80 to 75 MILLION YEARS AGO

Scientists found an Edmontosaurus fossil with T. rex teeth marks in it.

Edmontosaurus

(ed-MON-toe-sor-us)

Edmontosaurus grazed on all four legs. It nibbled on shrubs and trees like a giant deer. It was slow moving. And it was always on the lookout. A predator could be just over the hill.

FEATURE FACTS

WEIGHT
up to 7,000 pounds (3,175 kg)

LENGTH
30 to 44 feet (9 to 13 m)

LIVED
76 to 65 million years ago

Lambeosaurus

(lam-be-oh-SOR-us)

Lambeosaurus is known for its **hatchet**-shaped crest. Scientists aren't sure how these dinosaurs used their crests. The crests might have been for making sounds. Some people think the crest helped their sense of smell.

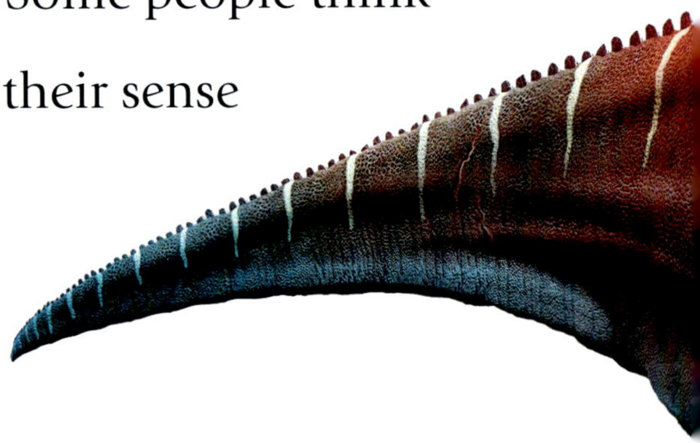

FEATURE FACTS

LENGTH	about 30 FEET (9 M)
WEIGHT	about 10,000 POUNDS (4,536 KG)
LIVED	76 to 74 MILLION YEARS AGO

Lambeosaurus' mouth had at least 100 teeth. Like all duck-bills, they wore out their teeth grinding plants. They grew new teeth as old ones fell out.

PREDATORS!

Duck-billed dinosaurs had to be on the lookout for these predators.

TYRANNOSAURUS REX

GORGOSAURUS

DASPLETOSAURUS

ALBERTOSAURUS

Parasaurolophus

(pa-ra-saw-ROL-off-us)

Parasaurolophus is known for its huge crest. This dinosaur blasted air through its crest. The sound might have been like a **foghorn**.

Like many duck-bills, this dino rose up on its hind legs to reach food. It could also run on two legs. Running fast helped it escape hungry meat eaters.

FEATURE FACTS

WEIGHT	LENGTH	LIVED
up to 8,000 pounds (3,629 kg)	30 to 35 feet (9 to 11 m)	76 to 74 million years ago

Its crest was longer than a hockey stick.

Bactrosaurus

(BAK-tro-sor-us)

Bactrosaurus lived in the woods of what is now Asia. It had a line of spines on its backbone. No one knows what the spines were for.

FEATURE FACTS

WEIGHT
about 3,000 pounds (1,361 kg)

LENGTH
about 20 feet (6 m)

LIVED
84 to 71 million years ago

Corythosaurus

(koh-rith-OH-sor-us)

Like many duck-bills, scientists think Corythosaurus lived in a herd. Group members ate and slept together. They traveled together. Big groups were better protected from predators.

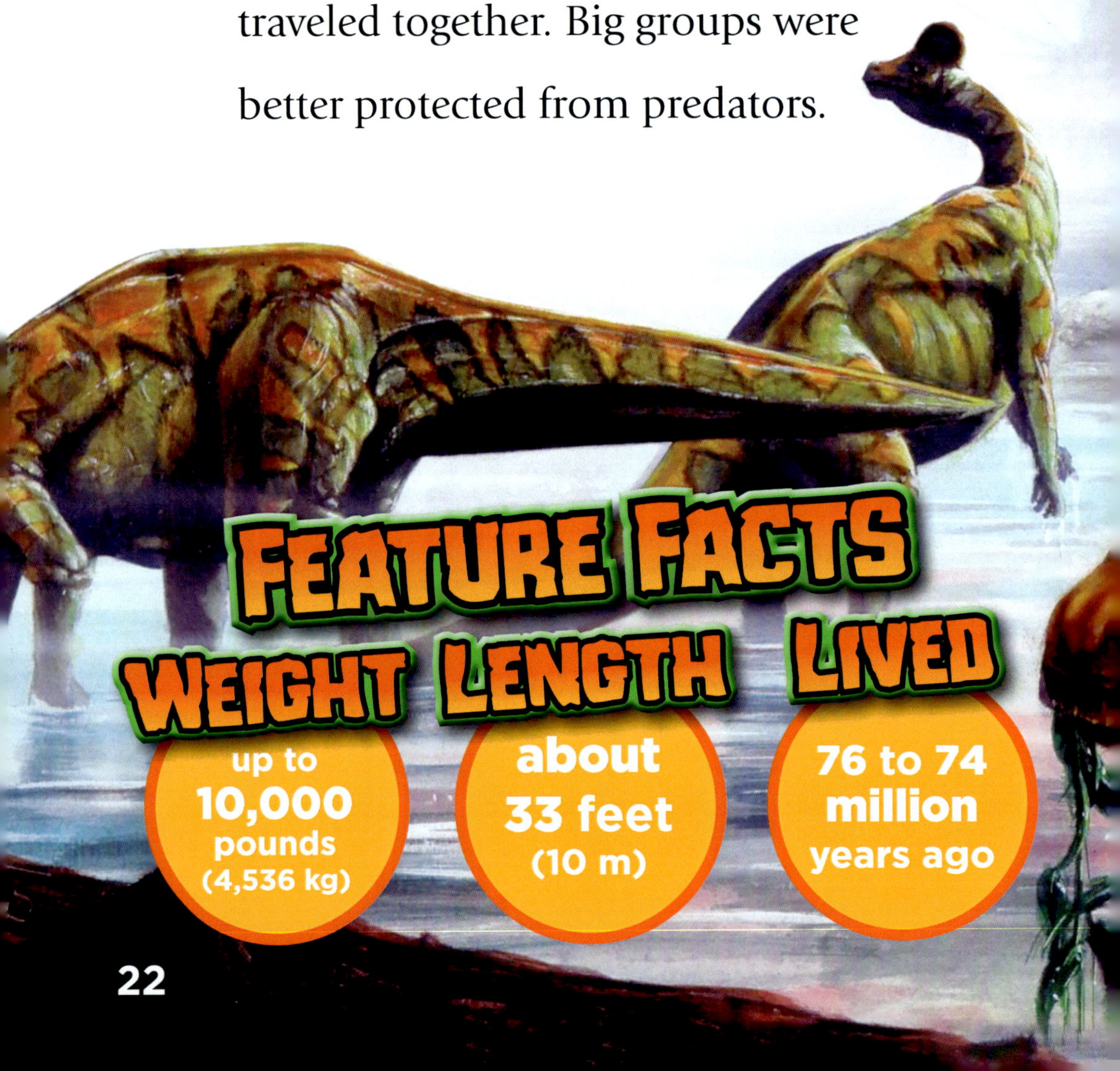

Scientists think Corythosaurus **migrated.** They used their crests to honk. The sounds helped members stay together.

Shantungosaurus had 1,500 tiny teeth.

Shantungosaurus

(shan-TUN-goh-sor-us)

Shantungosaurus was probably the largest duck-bill that ever lived. But aside from its size, it was like most other duck-bills. It had long back legs. Its tail was stiff. It ate plants. To protect itself, it lived in a herd.

FEATURE FACTS

LENGTH	up to 50 FEET (15 M)	LIVED 78 to 74 MILLION YEARS AGO
WEIGHT	up to 32,000 POUNDS (14,515 KG)	

CHAPTER 3

Gentle GIANTS

Duck-billed dinosaurs were gentle giants. They didn't have armor or spikes. But they were big and could probably run. Scientists are still learning about these amazing dinosaurs.

New research shows duck-bills grew faster than other dinosaurs. Duck-bills grew to huge sizes. Getting big fast would have helped young duck-bills survive.

COMPARE THEM!

Rank the dinos in this book. Then go find information on other duck-billed dinos. How do they compare?

LENGTH

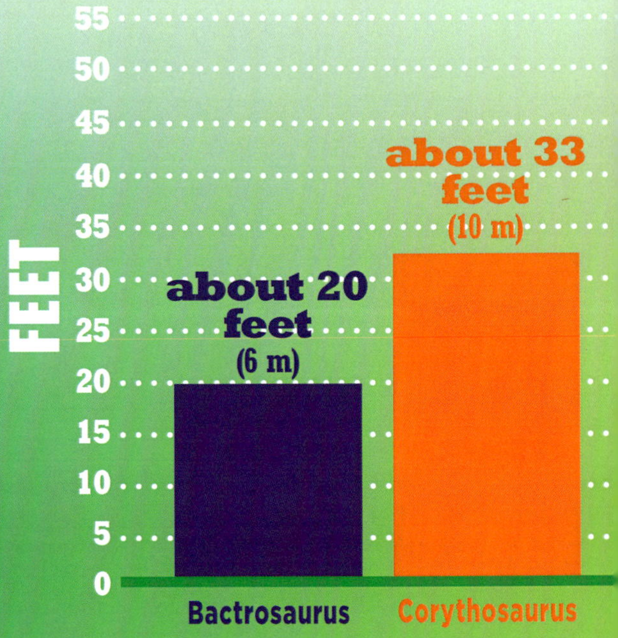

LIVED

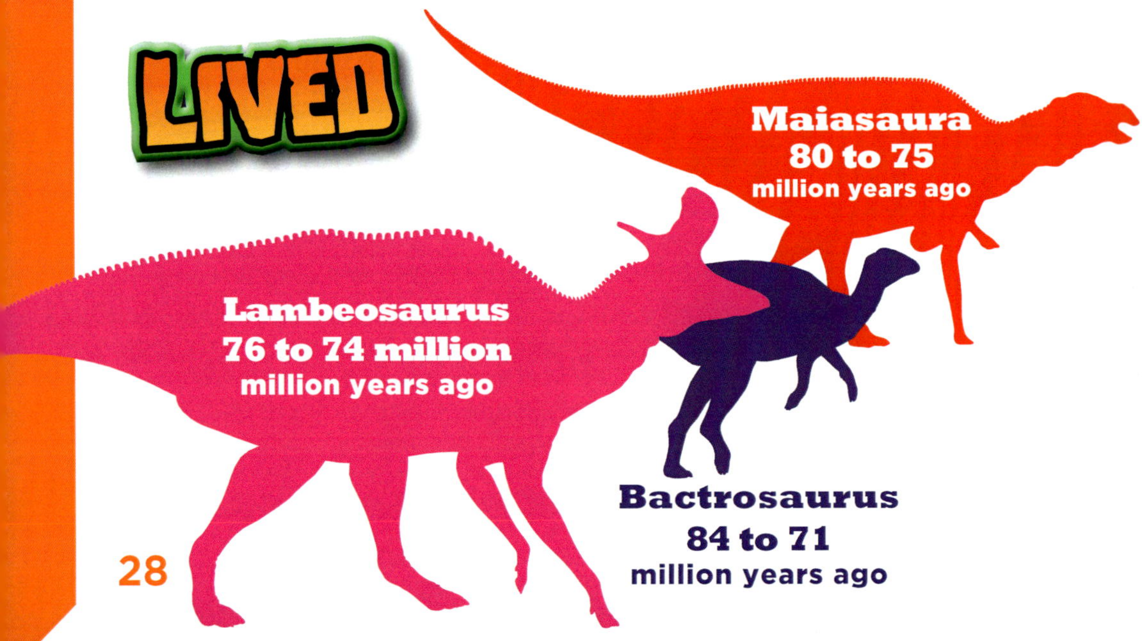

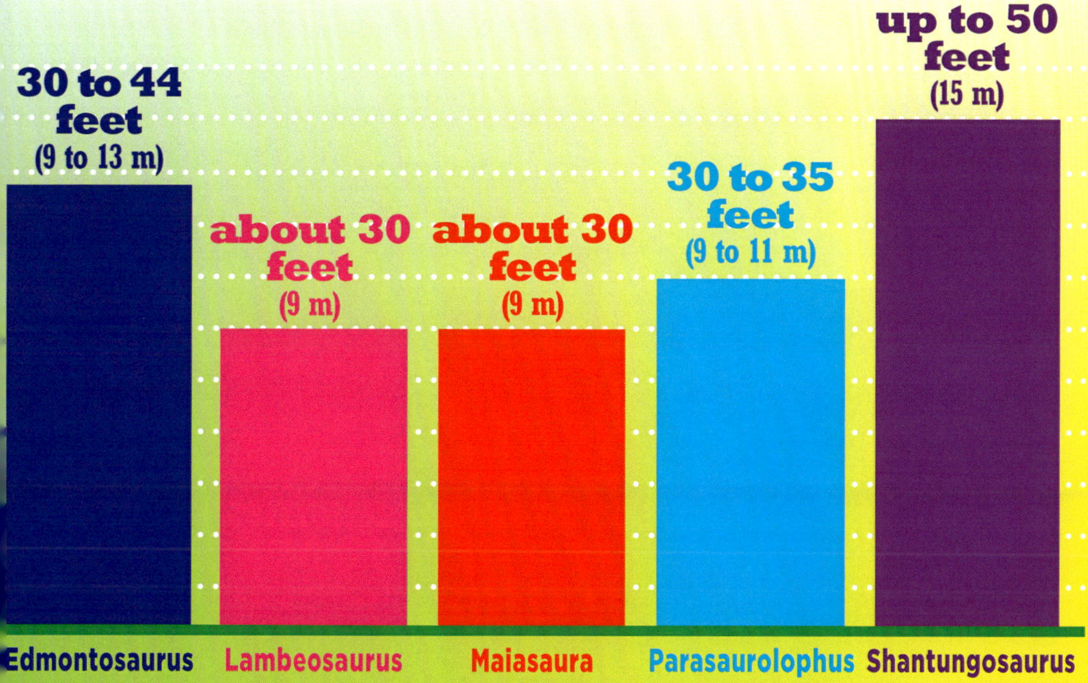
30 to 44 feet (9 to 13 m)
about 30 feet (9 m)
about 30 feet (9 m)
30 to 35 feet (9 to 11 m)
up to 50 feet (15 m)
Edmontosaurus
Lambeosaurus
Maiasaura
Parasaurolophus
Shantungosaurus

WEIGHT

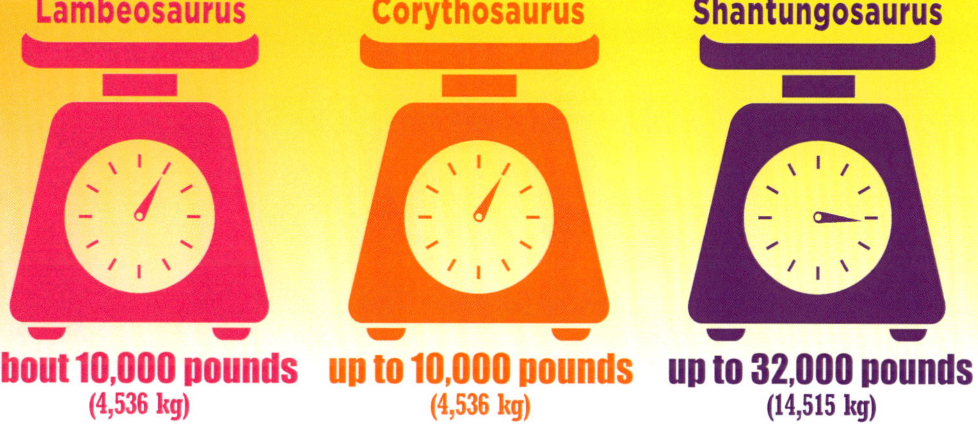
Lambeosaurus
about 10,000 pounds (4,536 kg)
Corythosaurus
up to 10,000 pounds (4,536 kg)
Shantungosaurus
up to 32,000 pounds (14,515 kg)

Cretaceous (kri-TAY-shus)—a period of time that was about 144 to 65 million years ago

foghorn (FAHG-horn)—a horn sounded in fog to give warning

fossil (FAH-sul)—the remains or traces of plants and animals that are preserved as rock

hatchet (HAH-chet)—a short-handled ax

herd (HURD)—a group of animals

migrate (MY-grayt)—to move from one place to another

predator (PRED-uh-tuhr)—an animal that eats other animals

survive (sur-VIV)—to remain alive

BOOKS

Lacey, Saskia. *Extreme Dinosaurs.* Amazing Animals. Huntington Beach, CA: Teacher Created Materials, 2018.

Peterson, Megan Cooley. *The Dinosaur Extinction: What Really Happened?* History's Mysteries. Mankato, MN: Black Rabbit Books, 2019.

Sewell, Matt. *Dinosaurs and Other Prehistoric Creatures.* Hudson, NY: Princeton Architectural Press, 2018.

WEBSITES

Dinosaurs and Prehistoric
kids.nationalgeographic.com/animals/hubs/dinosaurs-and-prehistoric/

Duckbilled Dinosaurs
kidsdinos.com/duckbilled-dinosaur/

Prehistoric World
www.nationalgeographic.com/science/the-prehistoric-world/

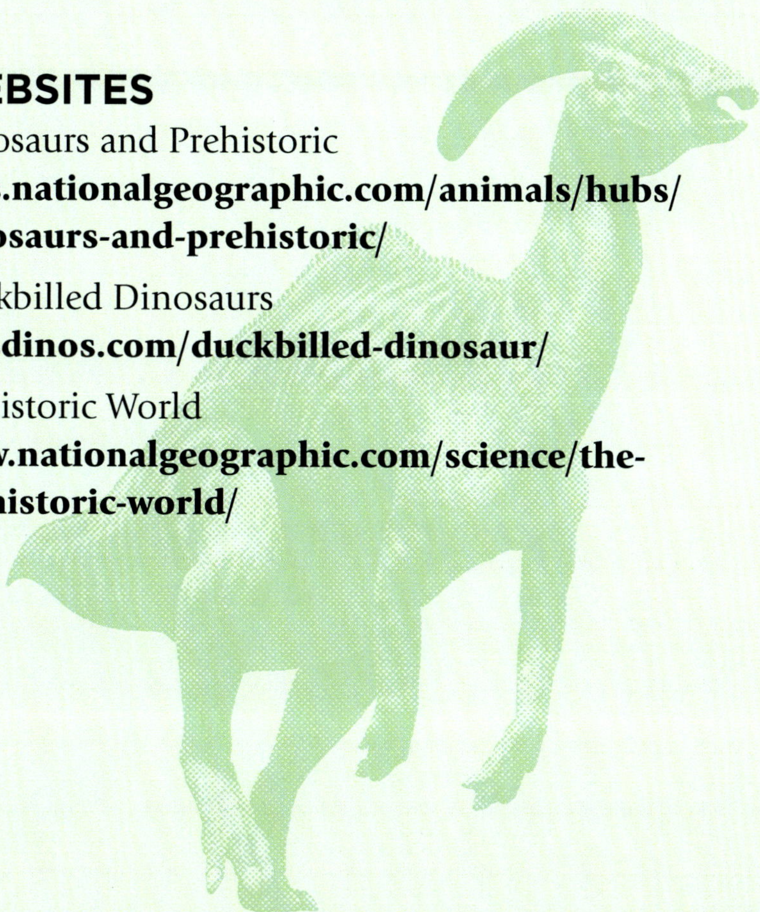

INDEX